ALSO BY WILLIAM JAY SMITH

◆ Poetry

Poems
Celebration at Dark
Poems 1947–1957
The Tin Can and Other Poems
New and Selected Poems
The Traveler's Tree: New and Selected Poems
Collected Poems: 1939–1989
The World below the Window: Poems 1957–1997
The Cherokee Lottery: A Sequence of Poems

◆ For Children

Laughing Time: Collected Nonsense
Boy Blue's Book of Beasts
Puptents and Pebbles: A Nonsense ABC
Mr. Smith and Other Nonsense
What Did I See?
Typewriter Town
Ho for a Hat!
Around My Room

◆ Criticism and Memoirs

The Spectra Hoax
The Streaks of the Tulip: Selected Criticism
Army Brat: A Memoir

◆ Translations

Poems of a Multimillionaire by Valery Larbaud
Selected Writings of Jules Laforgue
Collected Translations: Italian, French, Spanish, Portuguese
The Moral Tales of Jules Laforgue
(with Leif Sjöberg) *Agadir* by Artur Lundkvist
(with Leif Sjöberg) *Wild Bouquet: Nature Poems*
      by Harry Martinson

love poems
by
William Jay Smith

the girl in glass

woodcuts by
Jacques Hnizdovsky

BOOKS & CO.
A Turtle Point Press Imprint
NEW YORK

BOOKS & CO.
Turtle Point Press
New York

Certain of the poems in this collection appeared in *Poems* (The Banyan Press), 1947; *Celebration at Dark* (Farrar, Straus & Young), 1950; *The Traveler's Tree: New and Selected Poems* (Persea Books), 1980; *Laughing Time: Nonsense Poems* (Seymour Lawrence — Delacorte), 1980; *Collected Translations: Italian, French, Spanish, Portuguese* (New Rivers Press), 1985; *The World below the Window: Poems 1957–1997* (The Johns Hopkins University Press), 1998; *Here Is My Heart: Love Poems* (Little, Brown and Company), 1999.

The woodcuts by Jacques Hnizdovsky are reproduced by permission of Stephanie Hnizdovsky. Copyright © 1985, 2002 by Stephanie Hnizdovsky.

Design and composition by Melissa Ehn at
   Wilsted & Taylor Publishing Services, Oakland, California
Printed in Hong Kong

PUBLISHER'S CATALOGING-IN-PUBLICATION DATA

Smith, William Jay, 1918–
     The girl in glass : love poems / by William Jay Smith ; woodcuts by
Jacques Hnizdovsky. — 1st ed.
     p.   cm.
     ISBN 1-885586-59-0
     1. Love poetry, American.   I. Hnizdovsky, Jacques, 1915–1985.
II. Title.
PS3537.M8693G57   2002   811'.54
                                                          01-701195

LCCN 2001 132550

for
SONJA

Contents

THE GIRL IN GLASS

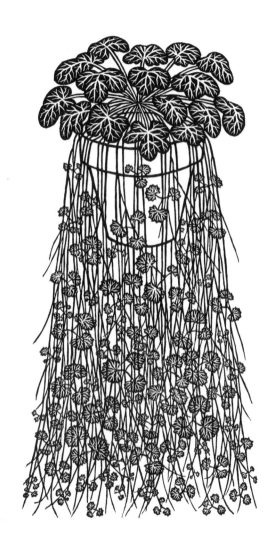

The Girl in Glass

Y ou've stood there long enough," I said,
  "Combing your hair. The pyramids
Are built; the traveler back
From ruined Thebes, Luxor, Karnak,
Has told the tale." You stopped.
And then, with fingers weaving,
Both white hands
Infiltrating copper strands
Of hair, began again.

Began, and then the delta sands
Ran out; you were a star-
Lit bloom, a water flower
Opening hour after hour
As I lay watching you in bed,
And the lamp burned low, and coral-red.

A mermaid in a fable wanted
To become a woman, and was nailed
With diamonds to my wall;
So Love, beside a waterfall,
Broke off a branch of berries from a tree,
And planted it at midnight
In the sea.

"You've stood there long enough."

The Young Lovers

These two went with cautious smile,
Edged with hope, a touch of fear,
Over a windy, whirling mile
Into a quiet sphere.

There to an island shaped with green
Corners descending to a shell
Holding a bay where silence fell
On reef and tree.

I saw them treading morning light
That seeped from sand, from palm
And bush, again at night —
Two shadows huge and calm

Stretched before the wave; I heard
Their cry like the cry of children who, in play,
Pursue a darting sky-blue bird
And find their bird at the end of day.

Night Music

The dark air rushes by us like a cry,
 Slowly the branches turn and twist and bend;
The stars, dim islands, sink into the sky,
Borne downward in a broad abyss of wind
That closes quietly to draw them under.
The night's deep water swirls and mounts and falls;
Rain descends in irons, and the thunder
Cleaves the thick charged air within these walls.

Now through the darkness will a careful prow
With chart and compass gain a scheduled place;
Now hands will calmly bend above a brow,
Now lips will lower to a trembling face;
And love within the constant mounting crests
Will break with equal fury from our breasts.

Roses Are Red

Roses are red,
Violets are blue;
The stars have the heavens
But I have you.

> Roses are red,
> Lilacs are mauve;
> You keep me sizzling
> Like a hot kitchen stove.

Roses are red,
Pinks are pink;
If I had a love potion
I'd ask you to drink.

Valentine Verses

I'll be yours, sweet cricket,
Till the sun freezes over
And the desert is flooded
And covered with clover;
Till it snows in the tropics
And camels wear socks;
And grandfather wristwatches
Are grandfather clocks.

The Lovers

Above, through lunar woods a goddess flees
Between the curving trunks of slender trees;
Bare Mazda bulbs outline the bone-white rooms

Where, on one elbow, rousing by degrees,
They stare, a sheet loose-folded round their knees,
Off into space, as from Etruscan tombs.

Unicorn

The Unicorn with the long white horn
　　Is beautiful and wild.
He gallops across the forest green
So quickly that he's seldom seen
Where Peacocks their blue feathers preen
　　　And strawberries grow wild.
He flees the hunter and the hounds,
Upon black earth his white hoof pounds,
Over cold mountain streams he bounds
　　　And comes to a meadow mild;
There, when he kneels to take his nap,
He lays his head in a lady's lap
　　　As gently as a child.

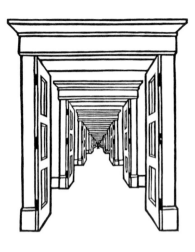

Cupidon

To love is to give," said the crooked old man.
    "To love is to be poor."
And he led me up his accordion stair,
    And closed his iron door.

"To love is to give." His words like wire
    Dragged the ocean floor.
"Throw ten of your blankets on the fire,
    Then throw ten thousand more."

His room was the prayer on the head of a pin.
    As clean as a diamond cut
Was the iron door which opened in
    And would not open out.

"To love is to give, to give, to give.
    Give more and more and more."
And the wind crept up his accordion stair,
    And under his iron door.

The Lady in Orange County

Beautiful lady, loops of country road
  In the County of Orange took me where,
Oh, my olive-backed sunbird, you stood
Greeting the bathers.

There was a freshness in your glance,
A freshness which the bamboo has perhaps
In its cool segments in the jungle shade.

The mountains knelt; cicadas made
Oriental music and you danced
Over the swaying grasses.

In autumn now returning to the shore,
I do not find the bathers; they have gone
To pick persimmons in the woods.

Beyond the holly branches where the clouds
Are touched with silver, and a bird
Dips in blood a red quill,

High on a balcony you stand,
And hear the galloping horsemen come
Out of the hollow over the hill.

The Ten

. . . one of the best-dressed ten women.
— A newspaper reference to Mme Henri Bonnet

Mme Bonnet is one of the best-dressed ten;
But what of the slovenly six, the hungry five,
The solemn three who plague all men alive,
The twittering two who appear every now and again?

What of the sexual seven who want only to please,
Advancing in unison down the hospital hall,
Conversing obscenely, wearing no clothing at all,
While under your sterile sheet you flame and freeze?

What will you say of the weird, monotonous one
Who stands beside the table when you write,
Her long hair coiling in the angry light,
Her wild eyes dancing brighter than the sun?

What will you say of her who grasps your pen
And lets the ink run slowly down your page,
Throws back her head and laughs as from a cage:
"Mme Bonnet is one, you say? . . . And then?"

The Diving Bell

Like one endangered in a diving bell
I move submerged, alone in the open sea.
Alive in love, I move in a lonely bell,
Driven alone into the open sea.

Immortal is the murderer who works my lines,
And all this air of heaven to no good;
Works me in loops, loops me in liquid vine
And takes me to his tangled water-wood.

Lost is the voice of the dark in dark dissolving,
Lost in the somnolent surf, the summer-swell.
I move in this world in such sonorous weather
On ocean bed I break from broken bell.

Martha's Vineyard

The valleys of this earth patrol the sky;
Her mountains are the mountains on the moon.
Below us here the first white flowers die;
They all will soon.

Greater than life is love, and cannot end
Even in immortality; we take
Dimension from the force which made the moon,
The earth, quake.

Like roses we have seen in early morning
Sweeping a stone wall, spilling upon the ground,
Love creates itself, or, dying small,
Accepts life's wound.

Don Giovanni in Campagna

Giovanni was a lumberjack;
He took delight in fallen trees,
A buxom wench, a smoking stack,
    The small amenities.

In stocking cap of engine red
And shirt of watermelon green,
He loved whatever lay ahead,
    And hated what had been.

Maple, spruce, and gentle pine
He sawed and hacked and hacked and sawed,
While buzzards grazed the timberline,
    And lean wolves crouched and clawed.

He cleared away the virgin trees;
With ax erect he proudly stood
On towering peak; an eerie breeze
    Stirred in the ravaged wood.

He could not move, he could not speak,
He breathed in dust and tasted fire;
The northbound freight's inclement shriek
　　Cut through the night like wire.

A buzzard—lank, suspended Z—
Lumbered, swooped; a redwood fell.
Earth divided: John could see
　　(Too late) the Pit of Hell.

Song for a Country Wedding

For Deborah and Marc

We have come in the winter
To this warm country room,
The family and friends
Of the bride and the groom,
To bring them our blessing,
To share in their joy,
And to hope that years passing
The best measures employ
  To protect their small clearing,
  And their love be enduring.

May the hawk that flies over
These thick-wooded hills,
Where through tangled ground cover
With its cushion of quills
The plump porcupine ambles

And the deer come to browse
While through birches and brambles
Clear cold water flows,
Protect their small clearing,
And their love be enduring.

May the green leaves returning
To rock maples in spring
Catch fire, and, still burning,
Their flaming coat fling
On the lovers when sleeping
To contain the first chill
Of crisp autumn weather
With log-fires that will
Protect their small clearing,
And their love be enduring.

May the air that grows colder
Where the glacier has left
Its erratic boulder
Mountain water has cleft,
And the snow then descending
No less clear than their love
Be a white quilt depending
From sheer whiteness above
To protect their small clearing,
And their love be enduring.

Narcissus

Narcissus.
Your fragrance.
And the depth of the stream.

I would remain at your edge.
Flower of love.
Narcissus.

Over your white eyes flicker
shadows and sleeping fish.
Birds and butterflies
lacquer mine.

You so minute and I so tall.
Flower of love.
Narcissus.

How active the frogs are!
They will not leave alone
the glass which mirrors
your delirium and mine.

Narcissus.
My sorrow.
And my sorrow's self.

[From the Spanish of Federico García Lorca]

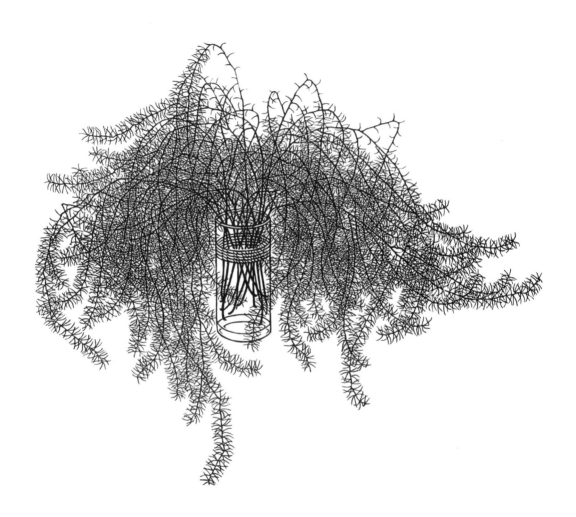

Venice in the Fog

For Sonja, con amore

I

Fog in mid-December has descended on Venice; and the city wraps
itself around itself

Like the sea horses we have seen in the aquarium, tails linked,
twisting, turning,

Rising gently to the green surface of the water; the water of
Venice, a mirror,

Is held up on all sides so that the bridge reflected rises and
drifts toward us, a twisted turret,

And the city, lighter than goose down, is about to float through
the air —

Or rest, a hulk, a battleship stranded, gray on gray sand, green
barnacles encrusting

Its gray guns; the silver of the mirror is rubbed away so that
one looks not into, but through, the glass,

And moves in a carnival, where black masks wander up and down,
    and the people wearing them

Are nowhere to be seen—they're lost in fog—and the buildings
    come at you through holes in the masks;

Bodies—ghosts' bodies—brush by you in the mist; the Bridge
    of Sighs is an eyelid

Lifted on a gray eyeball; and behind it a red boat light slowly
    streaks with blood.

II

St. Mark's bursts at us through fog, the mottled, humped face of
    a bright tropical fish;

The Doge's Palace beside it rests on the intaglio of its pillars,
    a stranded fish skeleton.

The *acqua alta* has subsided; in dim pools in the square the
    pigeons huddle in the cold,

Flying apart of a sudden like a fringe of wool, purple threads
    at their throats,

And one, frayed and battered, limps off toward the ruby glow of a
    jeweled shop,

And, nuzzling its head against a column, falls over dead, its
    mauve feathers the wet wisps of an old broom.

Fragments of buildings—architraves, cornices, pediments—fly
    through the night

And here at our feet, a group of gondolas tied together sit, squat,
    a row of black, muzzled dogs.

The lighted shops are so many bright boxes spilling out into the
    night—gold, glass beads

Falling beside the water like multiple chains from the throats of
    Venetian women.

Now in La Fenice—the fog behind us—we are inside the golden
    box, and below us women in Minoan dress

Sing out their lives, and fall spent on amber rocks . . . And now pink
    lobster, eel,

Layers of encrusted crayfish swim toward us through the gray
    light where streetlights drift,

The blue-pink pods of the medusa . . . And our forks come down
    upon the plate,

Cutting through the fog; we begin to bite into Venice, tasting
  its hidden, sea-green sweetness.

III

Three days and the fog gives no sign of lifting (after three days
  of fog it rains, they tell us) . . .

Cats go masked; white-veiled, bulging flower shops float off,
  barges bearing the remnants

Of bridal festivities . . . I touch their perfume as they move
  away; and from here in the room gaze down

On the bridge below and the shops beside it held in marbled water,
  veins of mist cutting

Through it while my pen on the page cuts through veined layers of
  consciousness . . .

Domes, arched windows rising toward me are bushes bent down
  with snow and ice; and the saints from their niches

Fly out like birds, all saying: Life is neither nightmare nor dream
  but dream and reality converging;

Heaven, as Blake knew, can be met with anywhere, and what
    cannot be seen must be imagined and seen more clearly . . .

Here seven years ago I walked at night through the fog, my steps
    echoing behind me;

My past life rose up unmasked before me; and even then I could
    see your face — a face I had not yet seen —

Swim toward me — a bright fine-boned face parting the spray
    before it, the figurehead of a ship . . .

And I gaze down now into the fog, and hear behind me — echoing
    up through my life —

Your steps on the stair; you come in, cold from your walk, and
    toss your purple cape on the bed, its fur wet from the fog;

Your hair falls red about your throat; you turn from the gold room
    and run the water in the bath,

Steam rising from it like fog; and below me footsteps echo on the
    pavement; bell buoys clang in the distance . . .

You step from your warm bath and lie down beside me; my hand
    moves over the nipples of your breast,

Down over the firm belly and rests on your thigh; as the mirror
  breaks in a thousand pieces,

The room is all pomegranate and gold; the fog clears — parting
  as if for the marriage of Venice with the sea —

And all that could not be seen is seen, all that was imagined, is, all
  that was lost, found.

Lovebirds

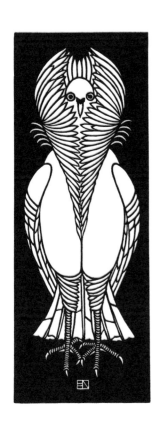

A bove finespun, unruffled sheets
    Bright agitated parakeets
Do not well, encaged, endure
The changes in room temperature.

Heraldic in unstable air,
They seem inclined, impelled to share,
Through active beaks, frayed, busy wings,
Intense concealed imaginings.

They gaze beyond hot coiling pipes
And waving cloth of zebra stripes,
Past thicket-green, plum-colored walls;
Ape incantations, and bird calls,

To where abed, with swift intake
Of breath, the couchant lovers wake,
Muscles tensing, eyes agleam,
Within the alcove's rising steam.

Quadruped, engaged, complete,
The bodies there grotesquely meet
Until with dumb, direct transaction
They end in mutual satisfaction.

Above the tumbling, milk-white sheets
The red-green ruffled parakeets
Do not chatter, do not sing,
But perch, head beneath one wing,

Nor lift their eyes and gaze about
Upon the scene of such a rout;
How can rumpled feathers measure
Such accomplishment of pleasure?

While sated lovers lie apart,
Each sullen still-ballooning heart
Wanders high above their bed
To say requited love is dead.

Love, indeed, no longer here,
Mushrooms into the atmosphere
Until by some celestial curse
It breaks upon the universe.

It breaks—and planets on their round
Wheel unconcerned above the ground;
Winds attack hunched apple trees
And furrow, snakelike, foaming seas.

The bed is made. The parakeets
Flash far away through tropic streets
In and out through black lianas,
Over broad sun-drenched savannahs,

Free and easy as the swing
And sweep of love's imagining
To where the temperature is even,
And the pure sunlight is all from heaven.

chrysanthemums

I had, here in the room before you came,
A dark delight announcing as with drums
Your coming, and the closing of the door,
Upon a tabletop, obese and tame,
These lion-headed flowers,
Four chrysanthemums.

A painter would have loved them, and been glad
To have them within reach: to see
Is mad, and madness teaches
Nothing if not love.
Great kings lay murdered in the flower beds:
I had, upon a table in this room,
Their four crowned heads.

In life we are often lonely, wanting death,
A kind of love not quite
Like this, a somnolence of light,
A glory which is native to the sun,
A poem in the landscape brooded on.

Dark springs, how dark;
And from the world's four corners, flowers
Like the heads of shaven Danes,
Huge and listless lions' manes,
Look down upon us where we lie
In darkness now, and overpowered die
Of love, of love.

Chairs above the Danube

Those two chairs were not really
all that ugly. Too bad the springs
protruded from them and the upholstery
was so hopelessly filthy.

But chairs they were, all the same. And right for that apartment.
So we carried them, mostly on our heads,
from Orlay Street across the former
Francis Joseph, now Liberty, Bridge,
to Number 2 Ráday Street where P. lived
at the time (as some of his poems will show).

A chair, not to say two, has
many uses. "Two Poets on a Bridge
with Chairs on their Heads"—one can imagine
a painting so entitled. I hope it would be
a down-to-earth painting and not one of those
transfigurations. Those two chairs—
and it's important to make this clear—were by no means
just halos around our heads. About halfway across the bridge—
and not for the purpose of proving anything—
we sat down on them. The springs protruded more prominently
        from
one—I don't recall which of us

got it. Doesn't matter since what happened later
can hardly be explained by that. It was a pleasant
summer evening. We lit cigarettes,
enjoying this one might say
unusual form of coziness.

                    The chairs later served
nicely for a while: at the P.s' they
were *the* chairs. But man wants something better
than what is: the chairs were sent to an upholsterer. Then the P.s
moved also, the first time, because they had to, the second,
because they hated their apartment. Nowadays
we meet less often at their place. Several things
brought this about: G. left A.
(P.'s wife) and then M. (B.'s wife)
broke off with me, and the other M. (G.'s wife)
divorced G. and married me (while the B.s
also separated) and P. attempted suicide and
has been living more or less in a sanatorium ever since,
not to mention the changes in the world situation,
so anyway: there's nothing left to sit on.

[From the Hungarian of Szabolcs Várady]

Cathay

You who have from far Cathay
    By perilous convoy come,
While under the spell of opium
    Or drunk with tea

In the palace of some paramour
    When day dies in the west,
Did you then gaze upon Princess
    Boudroulboudour

Whiter than luminous abalone
    In her black pantaloon;
And then one night beneath the moon
    Did John Chinee

Knock at your door, as bowed in grief
    As the asphodel of Ouac,
And vow he'd sew up in a sack
    His lovely wife

Who, though unfaithful, still was one
    Who could from wind-swept rock
Rise, a shimmering white peacock,
    In the rising sun?

[From the French of Paul-Jean Toulet]

Evening at Grandpont

Who under a stone bridge in the dark
Has seen? — We saw there, remember, wait,
The wind falls, wait, the street
Is empty now the leaves, the leaves
Are flocking to your feet —

Two swans, their floating, fluted necks
Down under feathers' whiteness,
Snow-plumed birds, awake? — No,
Not awake, two birds there deep
Down under thunder rocking,
Cradled, swans asleep.

Tell me, will you? — Well I know
How deep the swirling waters go
Beneath those two white throats,
The floor that whirls with dancer's step,
And death's dark notes,
Now tell me —

                 Who
Under a stone bridge in the
Darkness? — Wait, the wind, the columned air,
The leaves are falling, and they gather there
Like China's universities before the gate.

Black Girl

Yes, she is black. Her cheek has no rose tint,
  No burst of gold like grain against the sky.
Coal, too, is black. But light a match to it,
And into flaming roses it leaps high.

[From the French of Paul-Jean Toulet]

Helen

O Light, 'tis I, who from death's other shores
   Have come to hear the cold wave climb the stone,
And see again a thousand ships at dawn
Emerge from dark to the beat of golden oars.

And now these lonely arms call back from night
The kings whose salty beards amused my hands.
I wept; they sang of dim and conquered lands,
And the gulf their beakèd vessels put to flight.

The echoing conch I hear and the trumpet call
Answer the rhythmic blade in its rise and fall,
The slaves' clear song that holds the sea in chains.

And watch the gods, exalted at the prow,
With a classic smile the bitter salt wave stains,
Extend their sculptured arms, forgiving all.

[From the French of Paul Valéry]

Words by the Water

Beneath the dimming gardens of the sky
That ship, my heart, now rides its anchor chain;
A room is harbor when the world's awry
And life's direction anything but plain.
Still is the wind, and softer still the rain.
Sleep in my arms, my love. O sleep, my love.

Time hangs suspended: with its floating farms,
Its peacock-green and terraced atmosphere,
Now sleep awaits us, love. Lie in my arms;
It is not death but distance that I fear,
Dark is the day, and dangerous the year.
Sleep in my arms, my love. O sleep, my love.

A Pavane for the Nursery

Now touch the air softly,
   Step gently. One, two . . .
I'll love you till roses
Are robin's-egg blue;
I'll love you till gravel
Is eaten for bread,
And lemons are orange,
And lavender's red.

Now touch the air softly,
Swing gently the broom.
I'll love you till windows
Are all of a room;
And the table is laid,
And the table is bare,
And the ceiling reposes
On bottomless air.

I'll love you till Heaven
Rips the stars from his coat,
And the Moon rows away in
A glass-bottomed boat;
And Orion steps down
Like a diver below,
And Earth is ablaze,
And Ocean aglow.

So touch the air softly,
And swing the broom high.
We will dust the gray mountains,
And sweep the blue sky;
And I'll love you as long
As the furrow the plow,
As However is Ever,
And Ever is Now.

Roses

Accustomed as I am to certain flowers,
    I cannot quite make out what roses say.
But I have heard them speak; they spoke for hours
With a ho-di-ho (they did) with a ho-di-hey.

I heard them with a cock-a-doodle-doo,
And when I saw the sun, a cruiser, sink,
The Red Sea parted: we were cut in two.
Roses, being, perfect, do not think.

And yet it was with feeling that they spoke,
And with a fire so bright my body burned
That heaven, wheeling westward, spoke by spoke,
Was soon so wreathed in flames it barely turned.

Accustomed as we are, the roses said.
I looked into the dark, and, with one eye,
I saw a stem, a thorn. Come, let's to bed.
I love you more than red, red roses die.

The Wooing Lady

Once upon the earth at the midnight hour,
When all the bells are ringing in the wood,
A lady lies alone in a palace tower,
And yet must woo, and yet must still be wooed.

She glides upon the stair, a bird on water,
In costly sable clad, in seven sins,
To lie beside her knight, a king's white daughter,
A scullery maid beneath the marten skins.

The stars are out, and all the torches lit.
Below the window is an orange tree,
Catching the light and then returning it,
A juggler in an antique tapestry.

Horses gallop away; the boughs are shaken
So gently it can hardly be believed.
And over all the world the birds awaken
As he awakens, beautifully deceived.

Happiness

Sorrow is human, what of happiness?
The monster that is carved on Ishtar Gate
with fish-scaled back, bright eye, and clawed hind feet
is not so strange. And strange but not so sweet
the scent of violets in early spring
when newly rich, low-reaching branches sway,
and clear cold water bubbles from the sand
to bathe a carefree schoolboy's naked feet.

Yes, happiness is human: touch of hair
and hand; now where we go a trumpet vine
announces us upon a gilded stair;
and joy is real, and happiness is rare;
and so we kiss, and kiss again, and twine,
while roosters toss gold coins into the night.

Wedding Song

For Evita and Gregory

I would have instruments that could express
The captive music of clear mountain streams,
The shafted sunlight and the moon's cold beams,
A keyboard so attuned it could address
The songs recorded by your deepest dreams,
To speak for joy, keep discontent at bay
To wish you well upon your wedding day.

I would have baroque fountains cast in bronze
Where water would enclose with silver veils
Sea creatures half encased in virid scales,
And rising, fall, and rise against green lawns
In crystal iridescent peacock tails
Until each eye is dazzled by the spray
To wish you well upon your wedding day.

I would have pinewoods open to a sky
So spicy clear that you could touch the stars,
Lilacs rain-drenched to smell, and cool sandbars
To lie upon, rare pungent herbs to dry
And, memory compacted, store in jars,
And fireflies in a field of new-mown hay
To wish you well upon your wedding day.

I'd have persimmons picked within a glade
Where pheasant for your table moved among
Gold aromatic grass with berries hung,
Goose liver, pink as baby flesh, inlaid
With truffles that, dissolving, drug the tongue,
With salmon, oysters, wine in sweet array
To wish you well upon your wedding day.

I have only words but words are strong;
For if our senses are a kind of sieve
To filter out the rich life that we live,
Then from such riches words can shape a song
To offer up the joy that I would give
And to you thus the greatest wealth convey
To wish you well upon your wedding day.

Bachelor's-Buttons

Bachelor's-buttons are fine to see
When one is unattached and free,

When days are long and cares are few
And every green field sown with blue

Cornflowers that profusely seem
Attendant on a young man's dream.

Bachelor's-buttons are fine to see
When one knows no frugality;

And splendid to behold again
Lacing a jacket of gold grain,

A border tended by a wife
Who mends the fraying edge of life;

Who fashions in a hundred ways
Bright seams that cut through one's dark days;

Or will until buttons are counted and sold,
And the blue thread breaks, and earth is cold.

The Girl in the Black Raincoat

Thinking of you this evening,
   I think of mystery;
I think of umbrellas of crystal
Shading a cinnamon sea;
I think of swallow-tailed shadows
Enveloping history;
And the past becomes the future,
And the present is yet to be;
And life is a rain-swept mirror
Through which perpetually
A girl with bright hair flowing,
Dappled dark coat blowing,
Into the unknown, knowing,
         Walks with me.

A Picture of Her Bones

I saw her pelvic bones one April day
After her fall—
Without their leap, without their surge or sway—
I saw her pelvic bones in cold X-ray
After her fall.
She lay in bed; the night before she'd lain
On a mat of leaves, black boulders shining
Between the trees, trees that in rain pitched every which way
Below the crumbling wall,
Making shadows where no shadows were,
Writing black on white, white on black,
As in X-ray,
While rain came slowly down, and gray
Mist rolled up from the valley.
How still, how far away
That scene is now: the car door
Swinging open above her in the night,
A black tongue hanging over
That abyss, saying nothing into the night,
Saying only that white is black and black is white,
Saying only that there was nothing to say.
No blood, no sound,
No sign of hurt nor harm, nothing in disarray,
Slow rain like tears (the tears have dried away).
I held her bare bones in my hands

While swathed in hospital white she lay;
And hold them still, and still they move
As, tall and proud, she strides today,
The sweet grass brushing her thighs,
A whole wet orchard mirrored in her eyes; —
Or move against me here —
With all their lilt, their spring and surge and sway —
As once they did that other April day
Before her fall.

The Descent of Orpheus

A cockatoo with nervous, quick cockade
Consumes the cones upon a tree of fire
Whose branches cast a giant, trembling shade
Upon the earth, and on the gilded lyre
Of Orpheus, who wanders underground,
And is consumed, and is consumed by fire.

Hear him, O wild singer, as he moves
Below the helmèd hills:
"We cannot live like this, we must empty
Ourselves of living: we must go down
Through Death's blue acres to the roots of things,
Life's darker surfaces, where huge hot springs
Break from stone.
          We must seek Love
At the center of fire."
             And through a tangled wood,
Past triple-branching flame, he goes.

Knowledge which is powerful will take
Man down those worn rock ways
Below the ground, into the dark god's
Kingdom, fire-dominion:
He must learn,

Like Orpheus, he cannot turn
But turning find
His sweet love vanished, and descend
Where days are nothing, and dreams end,
And broad and burning rivers flow;
And yet must turn,
And turning, ask,
"What shall I do without her?
       Che farò?"

     And wanders on
Beyond all light,
From total darkness into night,
Bearing his flaming shield, his lyre.

Here at the cave's gray mouth,
The grave's green edge,
We watch the cockatoo, and cry: Return,
Return to us among the living.
       O so much
Is lost with every day: the black vanes
Turn in an angry wind, the roses burn
To ashes on a skeleton of wire;
Sun is mirror to the fire,
And earth, reflected, crumbles at our touch.

Saga

You will awaken me at dawn
  And barefoot lead me to the door;
You'll not forget me when I'm gone,
You will not see me any more.

Lord, I think, in shielding you
From the cold wind of the open door:
I'll not forget you when I'm gone,
I shall not see you any more.

The Admiralty, the Stock Exchange
I'll not forget when I am gone.
I'll not see Petersburg again,
Its water shivering at dawn.

From withered cherries as they turn,
Brown in the wind, let cold tears pour:
It's bad luck always to return,
I shall not see you any more.

And if what Hafiz says is true
And we return to earth once more,
We'll miss each other if it's true;
I shall not see you any more.

Our quarrels then will fade away
To nothing when we both are gone,
And when one day our two lives clash
Against that void to which they're drawn.

Two silly phrases rise to sway
On heights of madness from earth's floor:
I'll not forget you when I'm gone,
I shall not see you any more.

[From the Russian of Andrei Voznesensky]

Letter

Because a stamp will bear the damp
An envelope will bear a stamp.

Stamp and envelope unite
And fly together through the night

To reach the empty letterbox
A lean, uncertain hand unlocks.

Confronted with the cruel prose
Which stamp and envelope enclose,

Distraught, a young man bolts his door,
Paces up and down the floor

While metal rollers cross his brain
One hundred times, and then again,

Until as if congealed entire,
He kneels before a blazing fire

And sinks a knife into his heart.
Stamp and envelope depart:

Wet with tears, they rise in flame,
Leaving no address or name —

Only saffron ash that curls
Around dissolving blue ink-swirls,

Relinquishing to dark alone
Words written by the wind on stone.

The Battle of Tabu Tabu

A Tahitian Amatory Interlude

The Battle Wagon steamed into the bay
And Welcome was rolled out upon the mats;
The guns went off: Hooray! Hooray! Hooray!
And the flying fish were eaten by the cats.

The cocoa-colored ladies came our way,
Hibiscus at their ears instead of hats,
And little innuendo in their sway:
And the flying fish were eaten by the cats.

The Captain had his eye on Salomé:
The Second Mate, on looking through the slats,
Saw red—Ay! Ay! Ay! Ay!—and looked away:
And the flying fish were eaten by the cats.

The Battle Wagon steamed out of the bay,
The band pumped out Bye-Bye with sharps and flats;
The lobster sun was cooked a gunwale gray:
And the flying fish were eaten by the cats.

Envoi

For Heaven on this earth there's Hell to pay—
So on our burning deck this morning that's
Why all pricked out for every golden lei
Lie goldfish eaten by the flying cats.

On Parting

Time that is recorded is not now,
  Now when the train is leaving, and the clock
Is hooded in the distance, when the heart cries: How
Can you be leaving, for there is no time?

Some delight in the journey, in the crossing
Of accepted boundaries; you go
Knowing you love what's left, yourself, your loss
Of—
    Knowing the wheels will say, You do not know.

Rain is falling, and there is no rest.
Where are there tears enough to drown the sun?
Love also dies; the dead have loved you best:
Look for them there in the dark where the rails run.

Butterfly

Of living creatures most I prize
Black-spotted yellow Butterflies
Sailing softly through the skies,

Whisking light from each sunbeam,
Gliding over field and stream —
Like fans unfolding in a dream,

Like fans of gold lace flickering
Before a drowsy elfin king
For whom the thrush and linnet sing —

Soft and beautiful and bright
As hands that move to touch the light
When Mother leans to say good night.

Dachshunds

The deer and the dachshund are one.
—Wallace Stevens, "Loneliness in Jersey City"

The Dachshund leads a quiet life
    Not far above the ground;
He takes an elongated wife,
      They travel all around.

They leave the lighted metropole;
      Nor turn to look behind
Upon the headlands of the soul,
      The tundras of the mind.

They climb together through the dusk
      To ask the Lost-and-Found
For information on the stars
      Not far above the ground.

The Dachshunds seem to journey on:
      And following them, I
Take up my monocle, the Moon,
      And gaze into the sky.

Pursuing them with comic art
    Beyond a cosmic goal,
I see the whole within the part,
    The part within the whole;

See planets wheeling overhead,
    Mysterious and slow,
While Morning buckles on his red,
    And on the Dachshunds go.

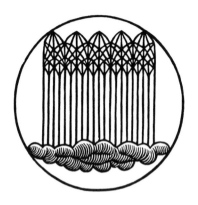

Immense and Red

Immense and red
Above the Grand Palais appears
The sun in winter
And then disappears
My heart like that sun will also disappear
Like it my blood will all drain away
Will go in search of you
Beauty
My love
And find you finally there one day
Where you will always be.

[From the French of Jacques Prévert]